Webster's Essential Literacy Skills

Grade 2 READING

By Troy Akiyama, Ed.D.

Created in Cooperation with the Editors of Merriam-Webster
and the Editors of Encyclopædia Britannica®

FEDERAL
STREET
PRESS

A Division of Merriam-Webster, Incorporated
Springfield, Massachusetts

This edition published by
Federal Street Press
A Division of Merriam-Webster, Incorporated
P.O. Box 281
Springfield, MA 01102
Visit us at: **www.federalstreetpress.com**

Publisher: Deborah Hastings
Art Director: Keith Plechaty
Editorial Director: Pamela C. Pia
Copy Editor: Sarah Chassé
Senior Editor, Encyclopædia Britannica, Inc.: Heather Campbell
Editor, Britannica Student Encyclopedia: Mary Rose McCudden

Definitions: *Webster's New Explorer Student Dictionary, Third Edition*

Federal Street Press books are available for bulk purchase for sales
promotion and premium use. For details write the manager of special
sales, Federal Street Press, P.O. Box 281, Springfield, MA 01102. For more
information email: sales@federalstreetpress.com

ISBN: 978-1-59695-109-9

1st Printing   Quad Graphics, Versailles, KY   8/2011

Printed in the United States of America

Contents

Let's get started!

Introduction

Dear Parents and Educators:

Welcome to the **Webster's Essential Literacy Skills** series. You have selected a unique workbook that will help improve children's reading comprehension, vocabulary, fluency, critical thinking, and test-taking skills. The 18 lessons within the workbook are based on the reading of nonfiction passages taken from the *Britannica Student Encyclopedia*. These passages can be found online in the Britannica Elementary Encyclopedia section of the *Britannica Online School Edition* at school.eb.com. The lessons in this workbook target the following nine essential literacy skills:

- Main Idea and Supporting Details
- Making Predictions
- Fact and Opinion
- Sequencing
- Cause and Effect
- Compare and Contrast
- Summarizing
- Asking Questions
- Drawing Conclusions

Designed by experienced educators, each workbook is aligned with the Common Core State Standards and includes pedagogically appropriate themes and concepts.

The **Webster's Essential Literacy Skills** workbook series provides easy-to-use lessons suitable for classrooms, homes, after-school programs, and tutoring sessions. Each lesson in the series helps build children's confidence and supports their reading success. Additionally, we have carefully selected high-interest topics and colorful illustrations to engage children and to nurture their lifetime love of reading.

Sincerely,

Deborah Hastings
Publisher
Federal Street Press

Common Core State Standards Overview

The lessons included in this workbook collectively address the Grade 2 **Common Core Reading Standards for Informational Text**. Refer to the appendix of this workbook for specific alignment information between the Common Core State Standards and the activity questions in each lesson.

Grade 2 Reading Standards: Informational Text

Key Ideas and Details	Ask and answer such questions as *who, what, where, when, why,* and *how* to demonstrate understanding of key details in a text.
	Identify the main topic of a multiparagraph text as well as the focus of specific paragraphs within the text.
	Describe the connection between a series of historical events, scientific ideas or concepts, or steps in technical procedures in a text.
Craft and Structure	Determine the meaning of words and phrases in a text relevant to a *grade 2 topic or subject area.*
	Know and use various text features (e.g., captions, bold print, subheadings, glossaries, indexes, electronic menus, icons) to locate key facts or information in a text efficiently.
	Identify the main purpose of a text, including what the author wants to answer, explain, or describe.
Integration of Knowledge and Ideas	Explain how specific images (e.g., a diagram showing how a machine works) contribute to and clarify a text.
	Describe how reasons support specific points the author makes in a text.
	Compare and contrast the most important points presented by two texts on the same topic.
Range of Reading and Level of Text Complexity	By the end of year, read and comprehend informational texts, including history/social studies, science, and technical texts, in the grades 2–3 text complexity band proficiently, with scaffolding as needed at the high end of the range.

More information about the Common Core State Standards can be found at www.corestandards.org

Using This Workbook

Overview

Research suggests that millions of adults lack basic English skills and that increasing childhood literacy is an urgent issue. Research also supports the teaching of essential literacy skills that provide the foundation for increasing reading comprehension, vocabulary, fluency, and critical thinking. The **Webster's Essential Literacy Skills** series targets nine literacy skills and strategies:

1. **Main Idea and Supporting Details**
   Students will learn to identify the main idea of a passage. Main ideas can be stated or implied and students need to delineate between the two. Additionally, students will identify the details that support or contribute to the main idea.

2. **Making Predictions**
   Students will determine what might happen next or what is implied based on the information presented in a passage.

3. **Fact and Opinion**
   Students will read passages and differentiate between objective statements of fact and subjective opinions.

4. **Sequencing**
   Students will determine the chronological order of events in a passage or the steps necessary to complete a task.

5. **Cause and Effect**
   Students will use nonfiction texts to identify an outcome (effect) and why it happened (cause). Additionally, students will understand that passages may contain multiple causes and effects.

6. **Compare and Contrast**
   Students will determine the ways in which two items or passages are alike and different.

7. **Summarizing**
   Students will use key ideas from a text to create a shorter version expressed in their own words.

8. **Asking Questions**
   Students will ask and answer questions to demonstrate a deeper understanding of a passage.

9. **Drawing Conclusions**
   Students will use stated information as well as their preexisting knowledge to determine what is also suggested or implied within a passage.

Getting Started

This section provides a framework for using this workbook with children. Advanced and experienced students can also complete these lessons independently or with a peer.

Prepare

Give your student the opportunity to look at the lesson's passages and pictures. Introduce the specific literacy skill (e.g., main idea and supporting details) to your student.

Practice

Read the "example" passage aloud to your student or have him/her read it to you. Talk about the passage and explain how the featured literacy skill relates to the passage.

Apply

Once you have introduced the skill and practiced using it with the "example" passage, have your student read the next two passages and complete the different activities independently.

Assess

After completing the lesson, have your student check the answer key to see how he or she did. Go back to the activity questions with your student to discuss why each answer is either correct or incorrect.

Extend

As an extension activity, you can ask your student to read other nonfiction texts and apply a specific literacy skill. For example, after completing the lessons on "cause and effect," you can ask your student to read an age-appropriate newspaper article and identify examples of cause and effect from the article.

Webster's Essential Literacy Skills: Grade 2 Reading • © 2011 Merriam-Webster, Inc.

Name_____

Farm Animals

The **main idea** is the most important topic in a passage. A **supporting detail** is a smaller piece of information that tells more about the main idea.

Example:

The horse is a mammal that people have valued for thousands of years. In the past people commonly used horses to get from place to place and to pull heavy loads. People still use horses in sports and for fun.

In this example, the **main idea** is that horses are valuable animals. The **supporting details** are that horses are used to get from place to place, to pull heavy loads, and for sports and fun.

Definition:

mammal (noun) a warm-blooded animal (as a dog, mouse, bear, whale, or human being) with a backbone that feeds its young with milk produced by the mother and has skin usually more or less covered with hair

Name_____

Read the passage and then answer the questions that follow.

The chicken is a bird that people all over the world raise for its meat, eggs, and feathers. It belongs to a group of birds called poultry.

Chickens have short wings and heavy bodies. This makes it hard for them to fly very far. Male chickens are called roosters. Roosters often have brightly colored feathers. They can be red, green, brown, black, or other colors. Female chickens are called hens. Hens are usually brown or white. Both males and females have one or two wattles. A wattle is skin that hangs from the throat. Male and female chickens also have combs. A comb is skin that sticks up from the top of the head.

Definition:

poultry (noun) birds (as chickens, turkeys, ducks, and geese) raised for their meat or eggs

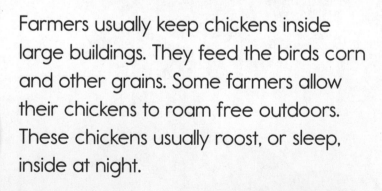

Farmers usually keep chickens inside large buildings. They feed the birds corn and other grains. Some farmers allow their chickens to roam free outdoors. These chickens usually roost, or sleep, inside at night.

Webster's Essential Literacy Skills: Grade 2 Reading • © 2011 Merriam-Webster, Inc.

Name_____

1. The main idea of paragraph one is: _____

_____

_____.

2. Which is **not** a supporting detail in paragraph two?
a. Female chickens are called hens.
b. Male and female chickens look different.
c. A wattle is skin that hangs from the throat.
d. Roosters have brightly colored feathers.

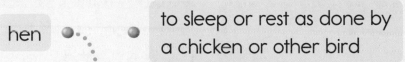

3. Match the vocabulary word with the definition.
Use your dictionary to help you.

hen ●   ● to sleep or rest as done by a chicken or other bird

rooster ●   ● the covering on the skin of a chicken or other bird; can be different colors

wattle ●   ● a female chicken

roost ●   ● skin that sticks up from the top of a chicken's head

comb ●   ● a male chicken

feathers ●   ● skin that hangs from a chicken's throat

Name_____

Read the passage and then answer the questions that follow.

Pigs are mammals that are known for their big appetites. Some kinds of pigs are wild, while others are domestic. Farmers raise domestic pigs for their meat, which is called pork, and their fat, which is called lard. The skin of pigs is made into leather. Their stiff hair is used for brush bristles.

A pig has a big body with short legs. It has thick skin covered with a coat of stiff hairs. Pigs are between 2 and 7 feet long.

Definition:

domestic (adjective) living with or under the care of human beings: tame

Webster's Essential Literacy Skills: Grade 2 Reading • © 2011 Merriam-Webster, Inc.

Name_____

4. The main idea of the passage is: _____

_____

_____.

5. One supporting detail from the passage is: _____

_____

_____.

6. Look at the picture of the pig, and draw a line from the picture to the name of each part:

tail •

legs •

• ear

• head

Name_____

7. The passage says: "Farmers raise domestic pigs for their meat, which is called pork, and their fat, which is called lard." Based on this sentence, what is one fact you learned about lard?

_____

_____.

8. Draw a picture of a pig. Use the passage to help you.

9. Write one detail you learned about pigs.

_____

_____

_____

_____.

Name_____

Ocean Animals

The **main idea** is the most important topic in a passage. A **supporting detail** is a smaller piece of information that tells more about the main idea.

Example:

Sea stars are animals that live in all the world's oceans. They have five arms and look like stars. For that reason they are often called starfish. But they are not fish. Fish have backbones, and sea stars do not.

There are about 1,800 kinds of sea stars. They can be brown, red, orange, pink, or other colors. Most sea stars are 8 to 12 inches across. A sea star's body has a disk in the center with five or more arms attached. Many sea stars can grow another arm if they lose one.

Definition:

backbone (noun) the column of bones in the back enclosing and protecting the spinal cord

In this example, the **main idea** is that sea stars are ocean animals that have five arms. Some of the **supporting details** are that they are not fish, that there are about 1,800 kinds of sea stars, and that many sea stars can grow new arms if one is lost.

Name_____

Read the passage and then answer the questions that follow.

Sharks are fast-swimming fish that have skeletons made of cartilage instead of bone. Sharks are among the oldest animals on Earth. The first sharks lived more than 300 million years ago. Today there are more than 300 types of sharks.

Definition:

cartilage (noun) tough flexible tissue that makes up most of the skeleton of vertebrates during early development and except for in a few places in the body (as the nose or outer ear) is replaced by bone

The whale shark is the largest living fish. It can grow to be about 50 feet long and weigh nearly 20 tons. The smallest shark is the dwarf lantern shark, which is only about 7.5 inches long.

Webster's Essential Literacy Skills: Grade 2 Reading • © 2011 Merriam-Webster, Inc.

Name _____

1. Draw a box around the main idea. Underline the supporting detail.

- Sharks are fish that have lived on Earth for millions of years.

- The first sharks lived more than 300 million years ago.

2. Write one supporting detail from paragraph one.

_____

_____.

3. What is the main idea of paragraph two?
   a. Whale sharks can reach 50 feet in length.
   b. Whale sharks can weigh almost 20 tons.
   c. Some sharks are very large, and some are tiny.
   d. Dwarf lantern sharks are only 7.5 inches long.

4. Draw a picture to show the main idea of the passage.

Name_____

Read the passage and then answer the questions that follow.

Whales are large animals that live in water. Whales may look like fish, but they are mammals. They breathe air and make milk for their young.

There are two kinds of whales: toothed and baleen. Toothed whales have sharp teeth and eat mainly fish and squid. Baleen whales do not have teeth. Instead, their mouths have something called baleen, which acts as a strainer. The baleen lets water out but holds in small fish, shrimp, and other creatures.

Definition:

baleen (noun) a tough material that hangs down from the upper jaw of whales without teeth and is used by the whale to filter small ocean animals out of seawater

Name_____

5. Write a sentence to describe the picture.

_____

_____

_____.

6. Draw a line to match each sentence with the type of information it gives.

The baleen traps food in a whalc's mouth. •

Toothed and baleen are the main kinds of whales. •

• main idea

Toothed whales eat mostly fish and squid. •

• supporting detail

Name _____

7. What is the main idea of the first paragraph?
   a. Whales are small.
   b. Whales are large animals that live in water.
   c. Whales breathe air.
   d. Whales look like fish.

8. Draw a picture to show one supporting detail from the passage.

Webster's Essential Literacy Skills: Grade 2 Reading • © 2011 Merriam-Webster, Inc.

Name _____

Explorers and Explorations

A **prediction** is a guess based on information from a passage or from something you already know.

Example:

Christopher Columbus opened the world of the Americas to Europeans. Columbus explored the area and brought more Europeans with him on later trips.

Columbus began an unstoppable wave of European settlement in the Americas. This settlement brought European culture to a different part of the world.

Definition:

settlement (noun) the act or fact of establishing colonies

By using information from the passage and personal knowledge, a reader might **predict** that Columbus changed the world in many lasting ways. A reader also might predict that Europeans faced many challenges as they settled in the Americas.

Name_____

Read the passage and then answer the questions that follow.

A submarine is a boat that can go underwater. Submarines are called subs for short. People use submarines to travel deep under the ocean's surface.

Militaries use submarines to protect ocean waters from enemies. Military submarines are usually very large. Scientists and explorers usually use smaller submarines. These submarines may have robot arms, cameras, and other tools to help scientists study the underwater world.

Definition:

explorer (noun) one who goes into or through for purposes of discovery or adventure

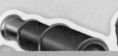

Name_____

1. Why do you think people would want to travel deep underwater?

_____

_____.

2. Circle the items a submarine might discover underwater.

3. Draw a picture of a small submarine that has robot arms.

Name _Keira_

Read the passage and then answer the questions that follow.

Humans have learned a lot about the planets, stars, and other objects by exploring space. Since 1957, more than 5,000 spacecraft have traveled into space to get information.

Humans cannot survive in outer space on their own. Astronauts bring their own oxygen with them. They wear heavy space suits for work outside the spacecraft.

Definition:

information (noun) knowledge obtained from investigation, study, or instruction

Name _Keira_

4. Write two things you think humans have learned by exploring space.

more about space   Histery

5. Draw a picture of one thing that a human might see from a spacecraft.

Name_____

6. Circle the picture of what an astronaut might wear outside a spacecraft.

7. Why do you think astronauts bring their own oxygen to space?
   a. because they have a lot of room on their spacecraft
   b. because there is no oxygen in space
   c. because their space suits are heavy

8. Write two other things an astronaut might take into space.

_____   _____

Name_____

Inventors and Inventions

A **prediction** is a guess based on information from a passage or from something you already know.

Example:

Thomas Edison was called a "wizard" because of his important inventions. He created more than 1,000 things on his own or with others. His best-known inventions include the phonograph (record player), the light bulb, and the motion-picture projector.

Definition:

invention (noun) an original device or process

By using information from the passage and personal knowledge, a reader might **predict** that Edison's inventions forever changed how people live. A reader might also predict that Edison invented more things than almost any other inventor.

Read the passage and then answer the questions that follow.

A railroad, also called a railway, is a type of land transportation. In a railroad a train moves along a path of two metal rails, or tracks. A train is a row of wheeled cars that are linked together.

Vehicles called locomotives pull most trains. A locomotive is powered by an engine that burns fuel or by electricity. In 1803 Richard Trevithick, a British engineer, built a locomotive that ran on steam power. Mining companies used it. In the 1820s another British inventor, George Stephenson, built the first steam train to carry things and people.

Definition:

transportation (noun) an act, instance, or means of carrying people or goods from one place to another or of being carried from one place to another

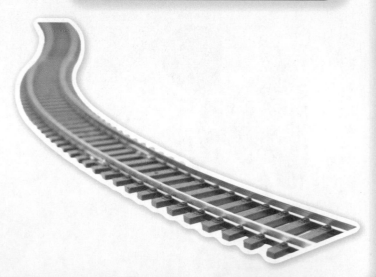

Name_____

1. Circle the picture of the type of transportation you predict is fastest.

2. Write two things you predict a steam train would carry.

_____   _____

3. Draw a picture of a type of transportation that you predict is faster than a train.

Name_____

Read the passage and then answer the questions that follow.

Television, or TV, is a system for sending moving pictures and sound from one place to another. TV shows give news and entertainment to people all over the world.

Definition:

entertainment (noun) something (as a show) that is a form of amusement or recreation

Inventors in Great Britain and the United States were the first to develop TV in the 1920s. The first working TV sets appeared in the 1930s. In 1936 the British Broadcasting Corporation showed the world's first TV shows. The first television stations in the United States started in 1941.

Webster's Essential Literacy Skills: Grade 2 Reading • © 2011 Merriam-Webster, Inc.

Name_____

4. Predict how people felt when they saw a TV show for the first time. Circle two words from the box below.

happy	sad	angry
sleepy	excited	hungry

5. Circle the TV you predict is older.

6. Draw a picture of what you predict televisions will look like in ten years.

Name_____

7. Write two sentences about what you think people did for entertainment before television was invented.

_____

_____

_____

_____.

8. Why do you think this TV has a handle on top of it?

    a. because it is from the United States

    b. because it is from Great Britain

    c. to make it easy to move

    d. to make the sound better

Name_____

Immigration

A **fact** is something that can be proven to be true. An **opinion** is a person's belief that cannot be proven to be true or false.

Example:

Ellis Island was once the first place that many people saw when they moved to the United States from other countries. People who go to a new country to live are called immigrants. Throughout its history the United States has welcomed many immigrants. Many of them arrived by boat at Ellis Island, which is located in a bay near New York City.

Definition:

arrive (verb) to reach the place started out for

"Ellis Island is located in a bay near New York City" is a **fact** because it can be proven to be true. "Ellis Island is a beautiful place to visit" is an **opinion** because it is a person's belief and cannot be proven to be true or false.

Name_____

Read the passage and then answer the questions that follow.

Asian Americans are people in the United States whose ancestors came from Asia. Many Asian Americans were born in Asia and later immigrated to the United States. Many other Asian Americans were born in the United States. Their families often have been in the country for many years.

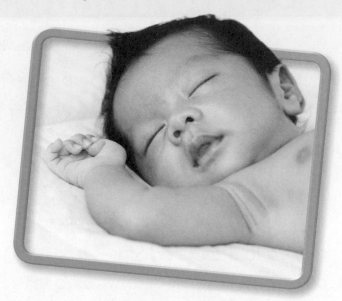

Definition:

roots (noun) the ancestors of a person or group of people

Asian Americans have roots in many different countries, including China, the Philippines, India, Vietnam, Korea, and Japan. Asian Americans have been an important part of the United States for more than 150 years.

Webster's Essential Literacy Skills: Grade 2 Reading • © 2011 Merriam-Webster, Inc.

Name_____

1. Which sentence is an opinion?

    a. Asia is a beautiful place to visit.

    b. Asian Americans have ancestors that came from Asia.

    c. Many Asian Americans moved to the United States from Asia.

    d. Some Asian Americans have come from China, India, and Japan.

2. Write one fact from paragraph two.

_____

_____.

3. Write an opinion about the picture.

_____

_____

_____.

Name_____

Read the passage and then answer the questions that follow.

Hispanic Americans are people living in the United States who are descendants of Spanish-speaking peoples. Hispanics have moved, or immigrated, to the United States for different reasons. Some have come to escape poverty and to find better jobs. Others have fled political problems and wars. Many Mexican Americans have ancestors who were already living in the Southwest before it became part of the United States.

Many Hispanics are proud of their roots. They want to pass their culture and the Spanish language on to their children. At the same time, Hispanics are an important part of U.S. society as a whole.

Definition:

descendant (noun)
someone related to a person or group of people who lived at an earlier time

Name_____

4. Draw a line between each sentence and its correct description.

Hispanic Americans have had different reasons for moving to the United States.

The United States is the best place to find jobs.

Hispanic Americans are descendants of people who spoke Spanish.

Hispanic Americans should be very proud of their roots.

• **Fact**

• **Opinion**

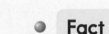

5. Draw a picture showing one or more facts from the passage.

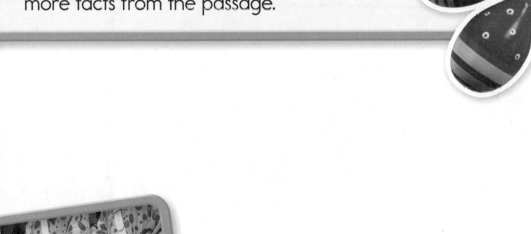

Name_____

6. Circle the fact and underline the opinion.

- Poverty is another way of saying very poor.

- Poverty makes everyone unhappy.

7. Look at the map. Circle the areas where the ancestors of Mexican Americans lived.

Name_____

Celebrations

A **fact** is something that can be proven to be true. An **opinion** is a person's belief that cannot be proven to be true or false.

Example:

Cinco de Mayo (5th of May) is a national holiday in Mexico. On that date in 1862 Mexican troops won a battle against the French. The Mexican people remember the event by listening to speeches and watching parades. In the United States, Cinco de Mayo is celebrated by people of Mexican descent. In many cities there are parades and events featuring Mexican culture and music, dancing, and food.

Definition:

celebrate (verb) to observe (a holiday or important occasion) in some special way

"Cinco de Mayo is a Mexican holiday" is a **fact** because it can be proven to be true. "Cinco de Mayo is the best holiday" is an **opinion** because it is a person's belief and cannot be proven to be true or false.

Name_____

Read the passage and then answer the questions that follow.

Thanksgiving is a yearly holiday marked by feasts and family gatherings. The day is celebrated in the United States, Canada, and other countries. It takes place on the fourth Thursday in November in the United States. In Canada it takes place on the second Monday in October. Both countries celebrate Thanksgiving with turkey feasts. In the United States, Thanksgiving Day parades and football games have become an important part of the holiday.

Definition:

feast (noun) a very large or fancy meal

Webster's Essential Literacy Skills: Grade 2 Reading • © 2011 Merriam-Webster, Inc.

Name_____

1. Draw a line to match each sentence with its correct description.

Thanksgiving dinner is delicious. ● ● **Fact**

Thanksgiving is a holiday. ● ● **Opinion**

2. Which statement is a fact?
a. Everyone loves Thanksgiving.
b. Playing football is the best thing to do on Thanksgiving.
c. The United States celebrates Thanksgiving in November.
d. Turkey is the best thing to eat on Thanksgiving.

3. Draw a picture showing something that people do on Thanksgiving.

Name_____

Read the passage and then answer the questions that follow.

People around the world celebrate the start of a year on New Year's Day. It is one of the oldest holidays. In Europe, North America, and South America most people celebrate New Year's Day on January 1.

On the night before, called New Year's Eve, people have noisy parties and big feasts. They stay up late and count down the seconds until midnight. Many people make New Year's resolutions because they see New Year's Day as a chance to make a fresh start.

Definition:

resolution (noun)
something decided on

Name_____

4. Draw a picture showing one fact from the passage.

5. Write an opinion about this picture.

_____

_____.

Name_____

6. Which word from the passage means "loud"?

_____

7. Circle the fact. Underline the opinion.

- January 1 is when many people celebrate New Year's Day.

- New Year's Day is a good time to make a resolution.

8. Write one fact from the passage.

_____

_____

_____ .

Name_____

Sports and Games

Sequence refers to the order in which things happen in a passage.

Example:

Basketball is a quick and exciting sport. It is very popular in the United States, where it began in the 1890s. In a basketball game two teams of five players compete. The goal is to score more points than the other team. They score by tossing a ball through a basket.

Play begins with a jump ball. A referee tosses up the ball between two opposing players in the middle of the court. The two players jump for the ball and try to tap it to a teammate. The team that gets control of the ball then tries to score points.

Definition:

compete (verb) to strive for something (as a prize or a reward) for which another is also striving

This example shows the correct **sequence** of events to begin a basketball game. The first event is that a referee tosses up the ball. Then, two players jump for the ball and try to pass it to their teammates. Next, the team that gets the ball tries to score points.

Name_____

Read the passage and then answer the questions that follow.

Electronic games are also called video games. People play electronic games on computers, in video arcades, and on home electronic game systems.

Definition:

quality (noun) a high standard: excellence

A man named William A. Higinbotham created one of the first electronic games, called *Tennis for Two*, in 1958. The first arcade game, called *Computer Space*, came out in 1971. More successful arcade games soon followed—for example, *Pong*, *Space Invaders*, and *Pac-Man*. The first electronic game system for home use appeared at about the same time.

The quality of electronic games improved in the 1980s, 1990s, and 2000s. Today Nintendo, Sony, and Microsoft are some of the leading makers of electronic games and game systems.

Webster's Essential Literacy Skills: Grade 2 Reading • © 2011 Merriam-Webster, Inc.

Name_____

1. Describe how to play your favorite game or sport in three steps.

First: _____.

Second: _____.

Third: _____.

2. Imagine how early electronic games might have looked. Draw pictures of the games invented in these years:

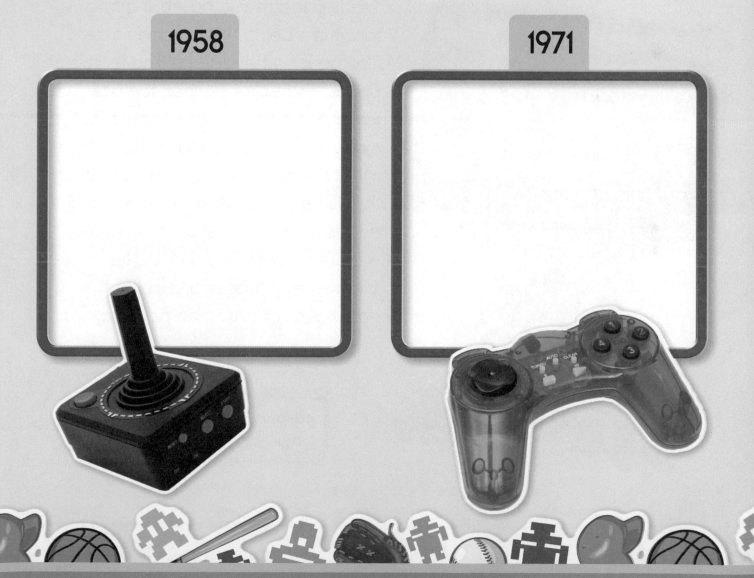

1958

1971

Name_____

Read the passage and then answer the questions that follow.

The sport of baseball has been called the national pastime of the United States. The game is played with a bat and a fist-sized ball. Two teams of nine players play against each other on a baseball field with four bases. The goal is to score the most points, which are called runs.

The two teams in a baseball game take turns being batters and fielders. Play begins when the fielding team's pitcher throws, or pitches, the ball toward one of the bases, called home plate. A batter standing at home plate tries to hit the ball out of the reach of the fielders. If the batter hits the ball, he tries to run to first base or farther without making an out. A batter scores a run when he goes around all the bases and returns to home plate.

Definition:

national (adjective) of or relating to an entire country

Name_____

3. What is the **first** thing mentioned about baseball in the passage?

a. The game is played with a bat and a fist-sized ball.

b. The goal is to score the most points.

c. Two teams play against each other.

d. Baseball has been called the national pastime of the United States.

4. Draw lines to show the sequence in which the following events would happen.

First •

Second •

Third •

• The batter runs toward first base.

• A batter hits the ball.

• The fielding team's pitcher throws the ball toward home plate.

5. Write what happens **before** a batter tries to hit the ball:

_____

_____

Name_____

6. Circle what happens **after** a batter returns to home plate without making an out.

The batter runs to first base.

The batter scores a run.

The batter hits the ball.

7. Number each picture 1, 2, or 3 to show what happens first, second, and third.

_____

_____

_____

Webster's Essential Literacy Skills: Grade 2 Reading • © 2011 Merriam-Webster, Inc.

Name_____

Works of Art

Sequence refers to the order in which things happen in a passage.

Example:

Sculpture is a type of art created in three dimensions—length, width, and height. Clay has been one of the sculptor's main materials since ancient times. Clay is easy to get and to use. Once early peoples learned to make bronze, metals became a popular choice for sculpture as well. Sculptors today use these materials as well as many others, including plastics, fabrics, fiberglass, neon tubes, and even garbage. Today, concrete is also used for large outdoor projects. This is because it is cheap, hard, and long-lasting.

Definition:

ancient (adjective) of or relating to a time very long past or to those living in such a time

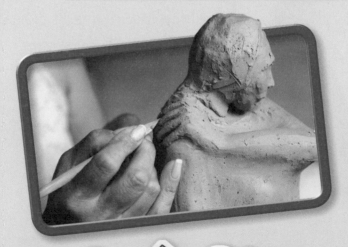

In this passage, we learn about different materials used over time to create sculptures. Clay was the first material used. Metal was the next material used. Lastly, sculptors today use many other materials, such as plastics. The order of materials used over time (clay, metal, and plastics) is an example of **sequence**.

Name_____

Read the passage and then answer the questions that follow.

Drawing is a form of art. To make a drawing, an artist puts lines on paper or another surface. Most artists start out by learning to draw. This is because drawing is the starting point for painting, sculpture, and other art forms.

Artists can choose from many tools for drawing. Pencils and pens are common drawing tools. Artists' pencils come in a wide range of hardness. Softer pencils make darker marks. Artists' pens may have different tips for making wide or thin lines. Some artists use special pens that they dip in ink before drawing.

Definition:

surface (noun) the outside or any one side of an object

Name_____

1. Draw lines to put the items in the sequence in which they appear in the passage.

First •

Second •

Third •

• Artists' pens may have different tips for making wide or thin lines.

• Most artists start out by learning to draw.

• Artists can choose from many tools for drawing.

2. Write down three steps that you would take to draw a picture.

First: _____

_____.

Second: _____

_____.

Third: _____

_____.

Name_____

Read the passage and then answer the questions that follow.

The art of creating pictures using colors, tones, shapes, lines, and textures is called painting. Humans have been making paintings for thousands of years. Paintings that may be 15,000 years old have been found on the walls of caves in France and Spain. Cave paintings usually show animals that early humans hunted.

Definition:

texture (noun) the structure, feel, and appearance of something

At least 4,000 years ago the ancient Egyptians decorated their tombs and temples with paintings. Later, people in ancient Greece painted their temples as well as vases and other objects.

About 1,000 years ago, during a period called the Middle Ages, artists in eastern Europe painted religious pictures on wooden panels. Meanwhile, the Chinese and Japanese created watercolor and ink paintings on long pieces of paper or silk.

Some 600 years ago, during a period called the Renaissance, European artists began to paint more lifelike pictures. They first watched the world around them. They then created new painting techniques.

Name_____

3. Which of the following is mentioned **first** in the passage?

    a. Japanese and Chinese artists painted on paper or silk.

    b. Eastern European artists painted on wooden panels.

    c. Paintings that may be 15,000 years old have been found in caves.

    d. Cave paintings usually show animals.

4. Draw a picture of a cave painting.

Name_____

5. Put these items in the correct sequence by writing 1, 2, or 3 next to each item.

_____ People created cave paintings.

_____ Renaissance artists created new painting techniques.

_____ Eastern European artists painted on wooden panels.

6. Draw three pictures to show three steps you would take to paint a picture.

First	Second	Third

Name_____

Native Americans

When something makes something else happen we call it **cause and effect**.

Example:

The first peoples in the Americas lived there for thousands of years before European explorers arrived. Descendants of many of these peoples still live in North and South America today.

The Pueblo Indians, the Navajo, and other groups lived in the dry Southwest, in what is now the United States. Peoples there learned to farm using very little water. Some built homes from stone and adobe. Others lived in simpler shelters.

Definition:

adobe (noun) brick made of earth or clay dried in the sun

In this passage, we learn that the Pueblo Indians lived in a dry area (the **cause**), so they learned to farm using very little water (the **effect**). This is just one example of **cause and effect**.

Name_____

Read the passage and then answer the questions that follow.

The Plains Indians include many groups of Native Americans who lived in the Great Plains area between the Mississippi River and the Rocky Mountains. For many years, Indians on the plains hunted buffalo (bison) on foot. Later, the Plains Indians got horses that were first brought to the New World by the Spanish. Plains hunters on horseback were able to travel farther than before in search of buffalo and then kill the animals more efficiently.

Definition:

efficient (adjective)
capable of bringing about a desired result with little waste (as of time or energy)

Name_____

1. Read the **cause** and write the **effect**.
Cause: Plains Indians did not have horses.

Effect: _____.

2. Read the two **effects** and write the correct **cause**.

Plains Indians were able to travel farther than before.

Plains Indians were able to kill buffalo more efficiently.

Name_____

Read the passage and then answer the questions that follow.

The Eskimo are native people of the Arctic regions. They live in Greenland, Alaska, Canada, and eastern Russia. Europeans and others have called them Eskimo for hundreds of years. They have different names for themselves. In Canada and Greenland they prefer to be called Inuit. In Alaska they prefer the term Eskimo.

In the past, the Eskimo got almost all their food by fishing and hunting. They ate reindeer, seal, walrus, and whale meat. On water, Eskimo hunters traveled in kayaks, which are boats covered with animal skins. On land they rode on sleds pulled by dogs.

Definition:

native (adjective) born in a certain place or country

The Eskimo made homes called igloos from blocks of snow. They also built houses of stone or logs covered with earth. In summer they lived in tents made of animal skins. They wore clothing made from animal fur and sealskin.

The Eskimo of Alaska had early contact with Russians. Meeting new people changed the Eskimo way of life. In the 1800s and 1900s some Eskimo left the Arctic to work in towns and cities. Those who stayed began using new things such as guns, motorboats, and snowmobiles.

Name _____

3. For each **cause** below, choose the correct **effect** from the box. Write the **effect** next to its **cause**.

> The Eskimo made homes from blocks of snow.
>
> The Eskimo made clothing out of animal fur and sealskin.

Cause	Effect
The Eskimo lived in a very cold part of the world.	_____ _____ _____.
The Eskimo hunted different kinds of animals.	_____ _____ _____.

Name_____

4. The passage says, "The Eskimo of Alaska had early contact with Russians. Meeting new people changed the Eskimo way of life." Draw two pictures to show the effects that meeting new people had on Eskimo people's lives.

5. How would the lives of Eskimo be different if they lived in a very warm part of the world, such as a rain forest or a desert?

They would make houses out of _____.

They would wear _____.

Name_____

Time

When something makes something else happen we call it **cause and effect**.

Example:

People use time to measure how long it takes for things to happen. They also use time to describe how long ago things happened in the past. Time helps to describe when things may happen in the future as well.

NEW YORK   LONDON   ISTANBUL   NEW DELHI

Long ago, people all over the world made many types of clocks and calendars to keep track of time. But the time was different in every city. In the 1800s some people thought there should be one system of measuring

Definition:

system (noun) an orderly way of managing, controlling, organizing, or doing something

time so that everyone could agree about what time it is. This was important for such things as making schedules for trains and knowing when to go to school. In 1884 countries throughout the world adopted the time zone system that is still in use.

In this passage, we learn that people agreed to use one system for measuring time (the **effect**) because the time was different in every city (the **cause**). This is just one example of **cause and effect**.

Name _____

Read the passage and then answer the questions that follow.

A clock is something used to tell time. Moving hands on the face of a clock point to the correct hour, minute, and second. Many clocks are made to be beautiful and useful objects.

Mechanical clocks get their power from moving weights or springs. These parts are attached to gears, or toothed wheels. The gears are attached to the hands of the clock. As the gears move they move the hands. Another object attached to the gears keeps them moving at a regular pace. Mechanical clocks must be wound up to work.

Electrical clocks get their power from electricity instead of weights or springs. The electricity can come from a battery or from an electrical socket in a wall. Some electrical clocks have hands, as mechanical clocks do. Others have digital displays, where the hours, minutes, and seconds are shown as numbers.

Definition:

regular (adjective) steady in practice or occurrence: happening on or as if on a schedule

Name _____

1. From what source do mechanical clocks get power?
   a. the sun
   b. moving weights or springs
   c. batteries

2. Pick the correct effect from the box and write it on the blank line to complete the sentence.

the clock to be beautiful   the hands to move   the clock to stop

The moving gears in a mechanical clock cause _____

_____.

3. If a mechanical clock is not wound up, what will happen?
   a. Time will speed up.
   b. The clock will stop working.
   c. The hands will move slowly.

4. Draw a picture of a mechanical clock.

5. Draw a picture of an electrical clock.

Name_____

Read the passage and then answer the questions that follow.

Sundials are the oldest known objects for telling time. The surface of a sundial has markings for each hour of daylight. As the sun moves across the sky, another part of the sundial casts a shadow on these markings. The position of the shadow shows what time it is.

Definition:

markings (noun) shapes, symbols, or words on something

Name_____

6. What **effect** does the sun have on a sundial? Underline the correct answer.

It makes the sundial look old.   It makes a shadow on the sundial

7. Draw a picture that shows what causes a sundial to work.

Name_____

8. If there are no shadows on a sundial, what is the **cause**? Underline the correct answer.

The sun is bright.   The sundial's gears are broken.

The sun is not shining.   The sundial needs to be wound up.

9. Tell a family member or a friend how these two pictures are the same and how they are different.

Webster's Essential Literacy Skills: Grade 2 Reading • © 2011 Merriam-Webster, Inc.

Name _____

Flowers, Plants, and Trees

We **compare** things by looking at the ways in which they are *alike*. We **contrast** things by looking at the ways in which they are *different*.

Example:

A flower is the part of a plant that blossoms. Flowers produce the seeds that can become new plants.

A flower usually has four main parts. These are the calyx, the corolla, the stamens, and the pistils.

The calyx is the outer part of a flower. It is made up of sepals. The sepals are usually green and look like small leaves. The sepals protect the flower bud while it is growing into a flower.

The flower's petals form the corolla. Within the corolla are the stamens and the pistils. The stamens are the male parts of a flower. The pistils are the female parts of a flower.

Definition:

protect (verb) keep from being harmed especially by covering or shielding

The passage **compares** sepals to leaves by saying that they look alike. The passage **contrasts** the stamens with the pistils by explaining how they are different: the stamens are male parts, and the pistils are female parts.

Name_____

Read the passage and then answer the questions that follow.

Hundreds of thousands of different kinds of plants grow on Earth. Some plants are so tiny that people can hardly see them. Others are trees that grow as tall as skyscrapers.

Most plants have several things in common. They need sunshine, water, and air to grow. Also, they are not able to move around. Plants grow nearly everywhere on Earth. Most plants grow in soil. They get the water and nutrients they need from the soil. But some plants do not need soil. There are plants that float in water. A few types of plants live on and get their nutrients from other plants.

Definition:

nutrient (noun) a substance that is needed for healthy growth, development, and functioning

Name_____

1. Write down two ways in which most plants are alike.
Then write down two ways in which some plants are different.

	Plants
Alike	Example: Most plants need sunshine. a._____. b._____.
Different	Example: Some plants are very tiny. a._____. b._____.

2. Draw pictures of two different plants.

Name_____

Read the passage and then answer the questions that follow.

Trees are tall, woody plants. They usually have stems called trunks. Trees are the largest and oldest living things on Earth. Some trees live for hundreds or even thousands of years.

Definition:

reproduce (verb) to produce another living thing of the same kind

Scientists divide trees into groups based on how they reproduce. Some trees reproduce with spores, or particles that grow into new plants. Most trees reproduce with seeds. Some seed-bearing trees grow their seeds in cones. Most seed-bearing trees grow their seeds in fruits or pods.

Scientists also group trees based on whether they lose their leaves. Trees that keep their leaves year-round are called evergreens. Trees that lose their leaves during the winter are called deciduous trees.

Name_____

3. **Compare** the many kinds of trees discussed in the passage. How are they all alike?

a. They all grow fruit.

b. They all are woody plants.

c. They all keep their leaves year-round.

d. They all grow cones.

4. **Contrast** trees that grow seeds with trees that reproduce with spores. How are seed-bearing trees different?

a. They are woody plants.

b. They grow spores.

c. They keep their leaves year-round.

d. They grow seeds in cones, fruits, or pods.

5. Draw two pictures of different trees.

Name_____

6. Compare and contrast evergreen and deciduous trees. Use the items from the box to help you complete the diagram.

- lose leaves during the winter

- keep leaves year-round

- need sunshine, air, and water

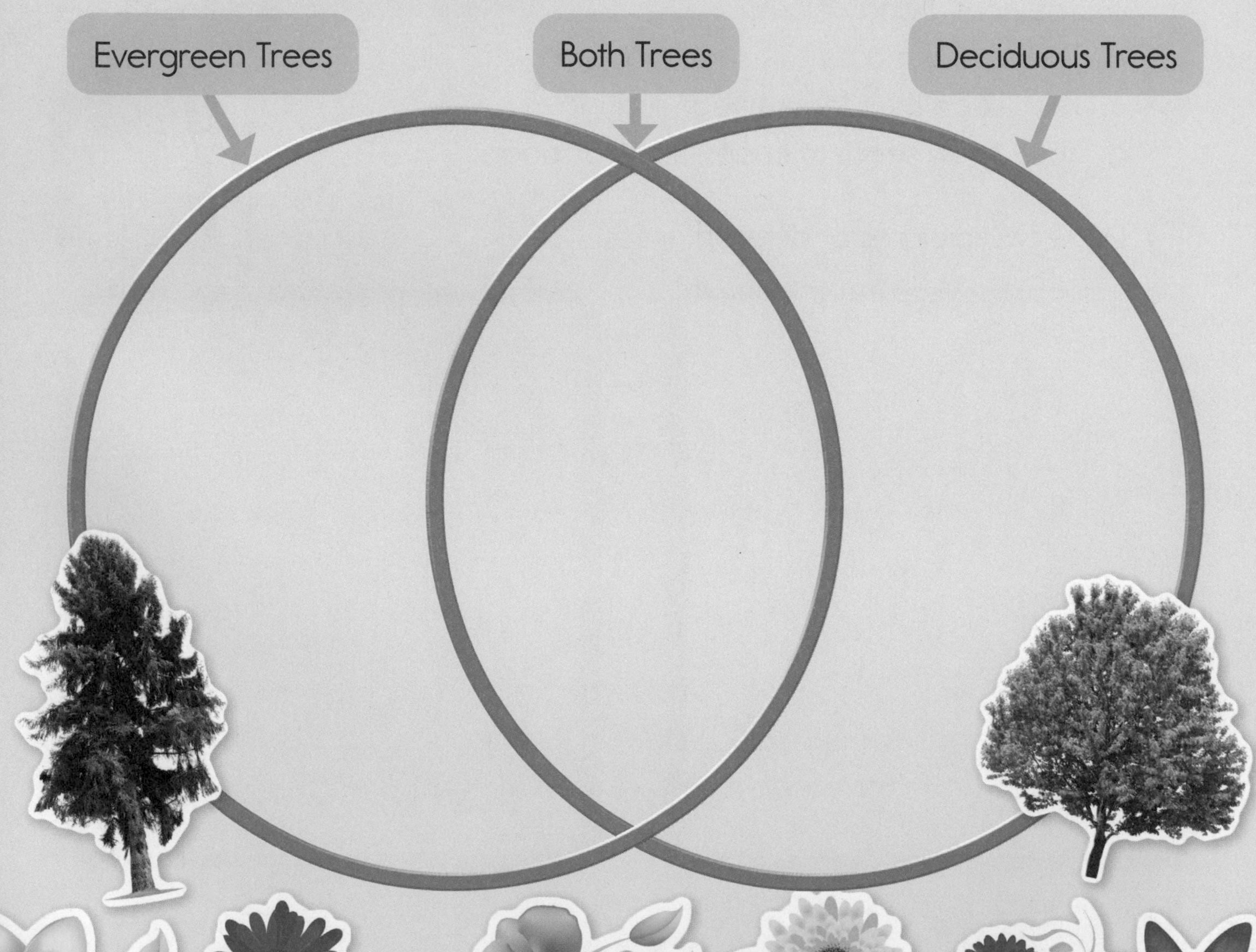

Evergreen Trees   **Both Trees**   **Deciduous Trees**

Name_____

Musical Instruments

We **compare** things by looking at the ways in which they are *alike*. We **contrast** things by looking at the ways in which they are *different*.

Example:

An object that can make music is called a musical instrument. A musical instrument may be as large as a pipe organ or as small as a tiny bell or whistle.

Definition:

vibrate (verb) to move or cause to move back and forth or from side to side very quickly

Percussion instruments make sounds when they are struck, shaken, scraped, plucked, or rubbed. Stringed instruments make use of stretched strings that vibrate when plucked, struck, or rubbed with bows.

If we **compare** the many musical instruments discussed in the passage, we see that they are alike in one important way: they all make music. For example, a pipe organ and a whistle are alike because they both make music.

If we **contrast** the musical instruments, we can find many differences between them. For example, a pipe organ is large, and a whistle is tiny. Or, stringed instruments have strings, while percussion instruments do not.

Name_____

Read the passage and then answer the questions that follow.

The basic stringed instruments in an orchestra are in the lute family. This means that the strings are stretched over a long neck that extends from the body of the instrument. These instruments include the violin, viola, cello, and double bass. The strings are rubbed with a horsehair bow or plucked with the fingers. Guitars, banjos, and sitars also belong to the lute family. They are played by plucking the strings with either the fingers or a small piece of plastic or metal called a pick.

Definition:

basic (adjective) relating to or forming the basis or most important part of something

Name_____

1. Circle the instrument that is most similar to a violin:

2. List one way in which the cello and the banjo are alike and one way in which they are different.

Cello and Banjo

Alike	
Different	

Name_____

Read the passage and then answer the questions that follow.

In a wind instrument, the sound is created by a stream of air that flows through or around the body of the instrument. In most cases the air comes from the player's mouth. In modern Western orchestras wind instruments are divided into brass instruments (made of brass or other metal) and woodwinds (made of wood or metal). Brass instruments include the trombone, trumpet, horns, and tuba. Woodwinds include the clarinet, saxophone, oboe, bassoon, and flute.

Definition:

modern (adjective) of or characteristic of the present time or times not long past

Name_____

3. Woodwind and brass instruments are alike because:
   a. both are made of brass.
   b. both are percussion instruments.
   c. both are made of wood.
   d. both are wind instruments.

4. Which instrument is most similar to a trumpet?
   a. a flute
   b. a saxophone
   c. a tuba
   d. an oboe

5. Draw a line to match each instrument in the box with the instrument below that is most similar to it.

Name_____

6. Compare and contrast brass and woodwind instruments. Use the items from the box to help you complete the diagram.

- air flows through or around them
- made of brass or other metal
- made of wood or metal
- saxophones
- trombones
- make music

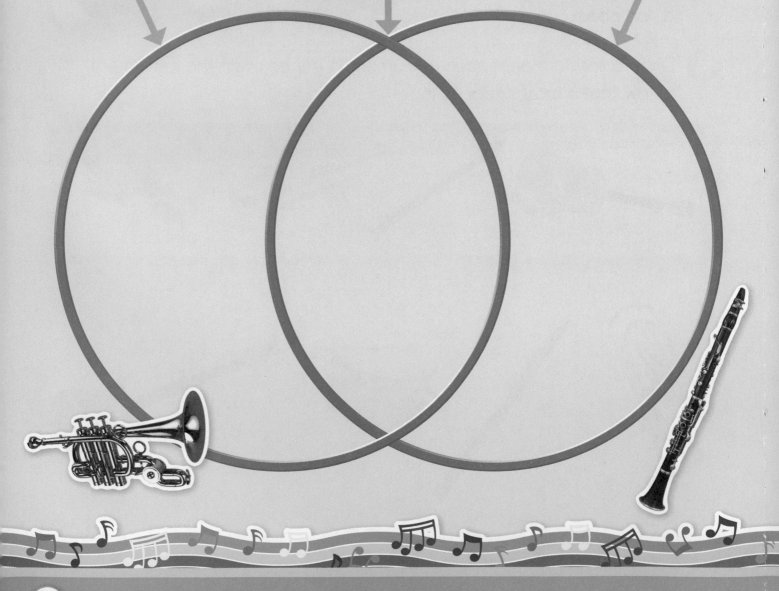

Brass Instruments   Wind Instruments   Woodwind Instruments

Name_____

Birds

Summarizing is when we use our own words to highlight the most important parts of a passage. Our retelling of the passage is called a **summary**.

Example:

Owls are birds that hunt and eat animals. Owls are active at night. Many stories have been told about their nighttime activity, quiet flight, and strange calls. Owls live around the world in almost every kind of habitat. Their length varies from about 5 to 28 inches. Most owls have brown, gray, or white feathers with streaks or spots.

Definition:

habitat (noun) the place where a plant or animal grows or lives in nature

A **summarization** of this paragraph would give the main information about owls in one or two shorter sentences, such as, "Owls are birds that hunt at night. They live around the world and come in different sizes and colors."

Name _____

Read the passage and then answer the questions that follow.

Crows are large birds with shiny black feathers. They often live together in large families. They are known for their loud voices and their intelligence. These clever, curious birds have been known to fly off with all sorts of little shiny objects, including people's car keys. Pet crows have even learned to copy human speech.

Crows eat a great variety of plants and small animals. Since they eat corn and other grains, they sometimes upset farmers. However, they also help farmers by eating insect pests.

Definition:

intelligence (noun) the ability to learn and understand

Webster's Essential Literacy Skills: Grade 2 Reading • © 2011 Merriam-Webster, Inc.

Name_____

1. Which sentence best summarizes paragraph one?
   a. Crows are birds that have large families.
   b. Crows like to steal keys and other shiny things.
   c. Crows are known as smart and curious birds.
   d. Crows are afraid of scarecrows.

2. Summarize paragraph two in one sentence.

   _____

   _____.

3. Write two sentences to summarize what you think is happening in the picture.

   _____

   _____

   _____

   _____.

Name_____

Read the passage and then answer the questions that follow.

Flamingos are tall, mostly pink birds with long legs. A flamingo often stands with its long, thin neck curved into an S shape. Flamingos fly and feed in large flocks of hundreds to more than a million birds.

Definition:

lagoon (noun) a shallow channel or pond near or connected to a larger body of water

Flamingos live in warm areas near lakes and bodies of water called lagoons. Flamingos feed while standing or walking in shallow water. They eat tiny living things such as algae and small animals such as shrimp and snails.

Webster's Essential Literacy Skills: Grade 2 Reading • © 2011 Merriam-Webster, Inc.

Name_____

4. Summarize paragraph one in one sentence.

_____

_____.

5. Which sentence best summarizes paragraph two?

a. Flamingos live in lakes and lagoons because they love the water.

b. Small animals like shrimp and snails live in lagoons.

c. Flamingos can eat while standing or walking through the water.

d. Flamingos live near shallow waters and eat small living things.

6. Write two sentences to summarize what you think is happening in the picture.

_____

_____

_____

_____.

Name_____

7. Draw a picture that matches the following summary of the passage: "Flamingos are long-legged pink birds that get their food from lagoons."

Name_____

Insects and Spiders

Summarizing is when we use our own words to highlight the most important parts of a passage. Our retelling of the passage is called a **summary**.

Example:

In many places the insects called fireflies can be seen on summer nights. Fireflies belong to the beetle family. They are also called lightning bugs.

There are about 1,900 types of fireflies. They usually like warm, humid areas, but some live in dry places. Fireflies make light with special body parts on the underside of their bodies.

Definition:

beetle (noun) any of a group of insects with four wings the outer pair of which are stiff cases that cover the others when folded

A **summarization** of this paragraph would give the main information about fireflies in one or two shorter sentences, such as, "Fireflies are insects that are usually found in warm areas. They have special body parts that allow them to create light."

Name_____

Read the passage and then answer the questions that follow.

Butterflies and moths are similar kinds of flying insects. There are about 100,000 types of butterflies and moths.

Butterflies and moths change forms during their lives. First, they hatch from eggs as caterpillars. Later, each caterpillar changes into a form called a pupa. The pupa lies still for weeks or months. Finally, the butterfly or moth becomes an adult with wings.

Definition:

similar (adjective) having qualities in common

Name_____

1. Which sentence summarizes paragraph one?
   a. Butterflies and moths are insects.
   b. Moths are flying insects.
   c. Thousands of different flying insects are called butterflies and moths.
   d. Butterflies change forms during their lives.

2. Summarize paragraph two in two sentences.

_____

_____

_____.

3. Circle the picture of what a butterfly looks like before it is a pupa.

4. Draw three pictures to summarize the steps in paragraph two.

Name _____

Read the passage and then answer the questions that follow.

Spiders are creatures with eight legs known for making silk webs to catch insects. They live everywhere in the world except for Antarctica. There are about 38,000 types of spiders.

Many spiders make venom, or poison, that they shoot into their prey. The venom of most spiders does not harm people. But a few spiders can cause pain and sometimes death in humans.

Spiders mostly eat insects. Some spiders are hunters that chase and overpower their prey. Other spiders make silk webs to catch flying insects.

Definition:

silk (noun) a fine fiber that is spun by many insect larvae usually to form their cocoon or by spiders to make their webs and that includes some kinds used for weaving cloth

Name_____

5. Which sentence best summarizes paragraph two?

   a. Most spiders use venom that is usually not harmful to humans.

   b. Spider venom can kill a human.

   c. Spiders shoot venom into their prey.

   d. Some spiders hunt, and others make webs to catch prey.

6. Write two sentences to summarize what you think is happening in the picture.

_____

_____

_____

_____.

Name_____

7. Draw a picture that summarizes paragraph three.

Webster's Essential Literacy Skills: Grade 2 Reading • © 2011 Merriam-Webster, Inc.

Name_____

Legendary Creatures

Questions usually begin with one of these words: who, what, when, where, why, or how. They always end with a question mark (?). **Asking questions** is an important part of reading.

Example:

Stories about unusual animals were common long ago. These creatures are called legendary because they exist only in these stories, or legends.

The dragon was thought to be a huge, scaly lizard or snake that breathed fire and had wings like a bat. Sea serpents were said to be huge snakes that lived in the deep sea. Mermaids were thought to have the heads and upper bodies of women and the tails of fish. The unicorn was described as an animal like a horse or a goat with a horn on its head.

Definition:

unusual (adjective) not done, found, used, experienced, or existing most of the time

As you read this passage, you might **ask questions**, such as:

- Has anyone ever seen a dragon?
- How could a mermaid breathe underwater?
- What would a unicorn use its horn for?

Name_____

Read the passage and then answer the questions that follow.

Many old Irish stories speak about small creatures with magical powers called fairies. Fairies are believed to have both good and bad effects on people's lives.

Definition:

creature (noun) an imaginary or strange being

Because fairies are said to have magical powers, some people think it is very foolish to risk upsetting them. Places where they might live or gather are treated with care and also some fear.

Name_____

1. Write two questions that you have about fairies after reading the passage. Do not forget to put a question mark (?) after each question.

_____

_____

_____

_____

2. What would you ask if you could speak with a fairy? Fill in the blanks with questions.

Why _____

_____

_____

_____?

How _____

_____

_____

_____?

Name _____

Read the passage and then answer the questions that follow.

Recent legendary creatures are the Loch Ness monster, the Abominable Snowman, and Bigfoot. Some people say that they have seen a monster swimming in Loch Ness, a lake in northern Scotland. The Abominable Snowman, or yeti, is a monster thought to live in the Himalayan mountains. Bigfoot, or Sasquatch, has been described as a large, hairy creature that looks like a human. Some people believe it lives in the northwestern United States and western Canada. No one has ever proved that these monsters are real.

Definition:

recent (adjective) of or relating to a time not long past

Name_____

3. Write two questions that you have after reading the passage. Do not forget to put a question mark (?) after each question.

_____

_____

_____

_____

4. Circle the creature that is believed to live in a lake.

yeti   sea serpent   Loch Ness monster   mermaid

5. Where is the Abominable Snowman believed to live?
   a. northwestern United States
   b. Himalayan mountains
   c. Antarctica
   d. western Canada

Name_____

6. Draw a picture of what you think Bigfoot might look like.

7. Fill in the blanks with questions about any of the creatures in the passage.

Why _____

_____?

How _____

_____?

Name_____

Medical Jobs

Asking questions is an important part of reading. Questions usually begin with one of these words: who, what, when, where, why, or how. They always end with a question mark (?).

Example:

Dentists are doctors who prevent and treat diseases of the teeth and gums. Tooth decay is the most common problem with teeth. Brushing and flossing the teeth can prevent tooth decay. But regular cleanings at a dentist's office are also important.

Definition:

decay (verb) to break down or cause to break down slowly by natural processes

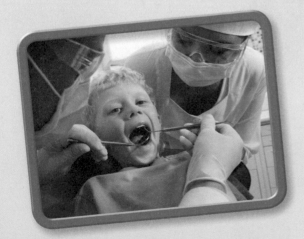

As you read this passage, you might **ask questions**, such as:

- Where do people learn to become dentists?
- How do brushing and flossing prevent tooth decay?
- Who was the first dentist in history?

Name_____

Read the passage and then answer the questions that follow.

Nurses make up the largest group of health-care workers in the world. They work with doctors to care for people who are sick or hurt.

Definition:

health (noun) the overall condition of the body

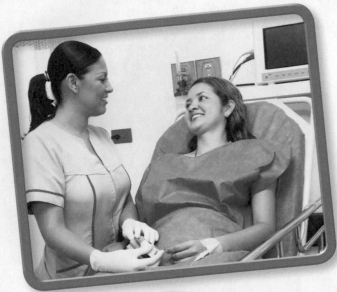

Nurses find out about a person's health by asking questions. They also check such signs as blood pressure and temperature. Nurses give medicine, change bandages, help sick people move around, and give other treatments. Nurses also teach people how to get well and how to stay healthy.

Name_____

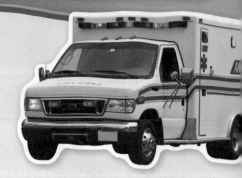

1. Write two questions that you have about nurses after reading the passage. Do not forget to write a question mark (?) after each question.

_____

_____

_____

_____

2. Draw a picture of a nurse at work.

Name_____

Read the passage and then answer the questions that follow.

Medicine is the science of keeping people healthy and healing the sick. Specially trained people called physicians, or doctors, practice medicine.

There are many parts to a doctor's job. Doctors first find out what is making a person sick. Then they decide on a way to help. They also predict when the patient will feel better. In addition, doctors try to prevent illnesses.

Definition:

prevent (verb) to keep from happening

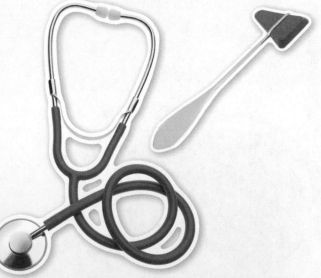

Name_____

3. Which of the following is **not** a question?

   a. What is another name for a physician?

   b. How do doctors find out what is making a person sick?

   c. Doctors try to prevent illnesses.

   d. Where do doctors usually work?

4. Draw a line to match each question with its correct answer.

Question:

               Answer:

Question	Answer
What is the science of keeping people healthy and healing the sick?	doctor
What is another name for a physician?	illnesses
What do doctors try to prevent?	medicine

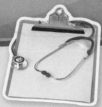

Name_____

5. Fill in the blank lines with questions that you would ask a doctor.

Why _____

_____

_____

_____?

How _____

_____

_____

_____?

6. Write one question about each picture.

   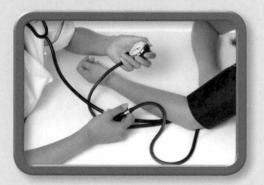

_____   _____

_____   _____

_____?   _____?

Name_____

The Solar System

When we read, sometimes we can learn more than what a passage says directly. We do this by combining information in the passage with what we already know. This is called **drawing conclusions**.

Example:

The solar system consists of the sun and everything that travels around the sun. It includes the eight planets, their moons, and many other things. However, even with all of these things, most of the solar system is empty space.

The solar system is only a small part of a huge system of stars and other objects called the Milky Way galaxy. The Milky Way galaxy is just one of billions of galaxies that in turn make up the universe.

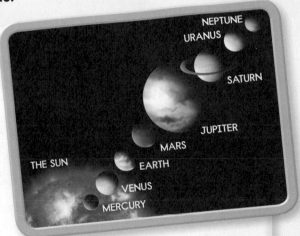

Definition:

galaxy (noun) one of the very large groups of stars, gas, and dust that make up the universe

You can use the information in the passage and your own knowledge to **draw conclusions**, such as:

- The solar system is very large.
- Earth is just a tiny part of the universe.

Name_____

Read the passage and then answer the questions that follow.

The sun is the star at the center of the solar system. It is a hot ball of gases that gives off a lot of energy. Life on Earth needs the light and heat from the sun.

Definition:

distance (noun) how far from each other two points or places are

The sun is the largest object by far in the solar system. The distance through its center is about 865,000 miles. This is about 109 times bigger than Earth.

Webster's Essential Literacy Skills: Grade 2 Reading • © 2011 Merriam-Webster, Inc.

Name_____

1. What conclusion can you draw about the sun?

   a. The sun is very important to Earth.

   b. The sun is cold.

   c. The sun is tiny.

   d. Earth is the center of the solar system.

2. Write a sentence to describe the picture.

_____

_____

_____

_____.

Name_____

Read the passage and then answer the questions that follow.

Planets are large natural objects that travel around stars. Eight planets move around the star called the sun. In order from the closest to the sun, these planets are Mercury, Venus, Earth, Mars, Jupiter, Saturn, Uranus, and Neptune.

Mercury, Venus, Earth, and Mars are rocky planets about the size of Earth or somewhat smaller. Jupiter, Saturn, Uranus, and Neptune are made up mostly of gases and have no solid surfaces. They are all much larger than Earth.

Definition:

gases (noun) substances (as oxygen or hydrogen) having no fixed shape and tending to expand without limit

Name_____

3. If you wanted to learn more about planets, which would be the most useful?
   a. a poetry book
   b. a science book
   c. a fiction book
   d. a math book

4. Circle the planet that is closer to the sun.

Venus   **Saturn**

5. Draw a box around the planet that is farther away from the sun.

Neptune   **Earth**

6. Draw a picture of a planet that is similar to Jupiter.

Name_____

7. Underline the planet in the box that is rocky and about the size of Earth:

| Jupiter | Saturn | Mars | Uranus |

8. Draw a picture of the solar system. Be sure to include, and label, the sun and the eight planets.

Name_____

Seasons

When we read, sometimes we can learn more than what a passage says directly. We do this by combining information in the passage with what we already know. This is called **drawing conclusions**.

Example:

As a year passes, we see regular changes in the weather. The cycle of weather changes has four parts, known as the seasons. The four seasons are winter, spring, summer, and autumn, or fall.

Definition:

cycle (noun) a period of time taken up by a series of events or actions that repeat themselves again and again in the same order

You can use the information in the passage and your own knowledge to **draw conclusions**, such as:

- We can expect to have four seasons every year.
- The weather cycle stays the same each year.
- Each season is about 3 months long.

Name_____

Read the passage and then answer the questions that follow.

During winter, the weather is usually cold and often snowy. Some animals hibernate, or sleep for a long time. Many birds have moved to warmer places. Some plants die, and others stop growing.

When spring arrives temperatures become warmer. Plants and trees make new leaves and flowers. Birds return from their winter homes, and animals come out of hibernation.

Definition:

hibernate (verb) to pass all or part of the winter in an inactive state in which the body temperature drops and breathing slows

Webster's Essential Literacy Skills: Grade 2 Reading • © 2011 Merriam-Webster, Inc.

Name_____

1. Circle the season that is usually colder.

winter   spring

2. Underline the item you are likely to see in the spring.

new leaves on trees   hibernating animals   plants that are dying

3. Write the season under each picture.

_____   _____

Name_____

Read the passage and then answer the questions that follow.

During the summer, temperatures reach their highest levels. There are more hours of daylight. This extra sunshine helps plants to grow.

Temperatures fall again as autumn begins. Some trees and plants lose their leaves. Animals with fur grow thicker coats to keep them warm during the coming winter. Many birds travel to warmer places.

Definition:

temperature (noun) degree of hotness or coldness as measured on a scale

Webster's Essential Literacy Skills: Grade 2 Reading • © 2011 Merriam-Webster, Inc.

Name_____

4. Draw a picture of something you might do in the summer.

5. Draw a picture of something you might see in the autumn.

Name_____

6. Look at the picture and circle the correct season.

summer   **autumn**

7. Circle the season in which you might see or use each item.

   summer

              autumn

   summer

              autumn

   summer

              autumn

   summer

              autumn

Answer Key

Lesson 1

Lesson 1 • Main Idea and Supporting Details   Name_____

1. The main idea of paragraph one is: __Answers will vary__

2. Which is **not** a supporting detail in paragraph two?
   a. Female chickens are called hens.
   b. Male and female chickens look different.
   c. A wattle is skin that hangs from the throat.
   d. Roosters have brightly colored feathers.

3. Match the vocabulary word with the definition. Use your dictionary to help you.

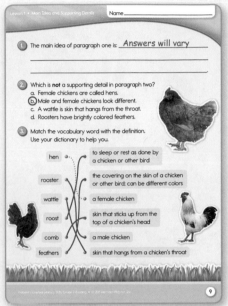

hen — to sleep or rest as done by a chicken or other bird

rooster — the covering on the skin of a chicken or other bird; can be different colors

wattle — a female chicken

roost — skin that sticks up from the top of a chicken's head

comb — a male chicken

feathers — skin that hangs from a chicken's throat

9

Lesson 1 • Main Idea and Supporting Details   Name_____

4. The main idea of the passage is: __Answers will vary__

5. One supporting detail from the passage is: __Answers will vary__

6. Look at the picture of the pig, and draw a line from the picture to the name of each part:

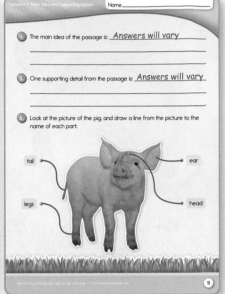

tail   ear

legs   head

11

Lesson 1 • Main Idea and Supporting Details   Name_____

7. The passage says: "Farmers raise domestic pigs for their meat, which is called pork, and their fat, which is called lard." Based on this sentence, what is one fact you learned about lard?
   __Answers will vary__

8. Draw a picture of a pig. Use the passage to help you.

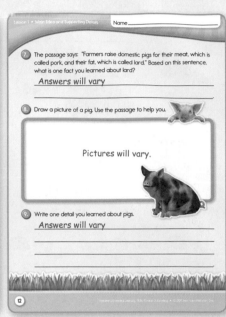

Pictures will vary.

9. Write one detail you learned about pigs.
   __Answers will vary__

12

Lesson 2

Lesson 2 • Main Idea and Supporting Details   Name_____

1. Draw a box around the main idea. Underline the supporting detail.
   - Sharks are fish that have lived on Earth for millions of years.
   - The first sharks lived more than 300 million years ago.

2. Write one supporting detail from paragraph one.
   __Answers will vary__

3. What is the main idea of paragraph two?
   a. Whale sharks can reach 50 feet in length.
   b. Whale sharks can weigh almost 20 tons.
   c. Some sharks are very large, and some are tiny.
   d. Dwarf lantern sharks are only 7.5 inches long.

4. Draw a picture to show the main idea of the passage.

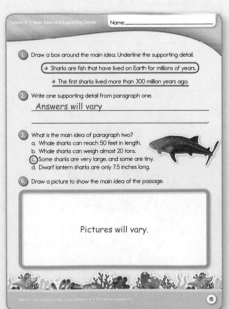

Pictures will vary.

15

Lesson 2 • Main Idea and Supporting Details   Name_____

5. Write a sentence to describe the picture.

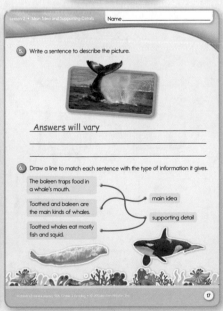

__Answers will vary__

6. Draw a line to match each sentence with the type of information it gives.

The baleen traps food in a whale's mouth.

Toothed and baleen are the main kinds of whales.   main idea

Toothed whales eat mostly fish and squid.   supporting detail

17

Lesson 2 • Main Idea and Supporting Details   Name_____

7. What is the main idea of the first paragraph?
   a. Whales are small.
   b. Whales are large animals that live in water.
   c. Whales breathe air.
   d. Whales look like fish.

8. Draw a picture to show one supporting detail from the passage.

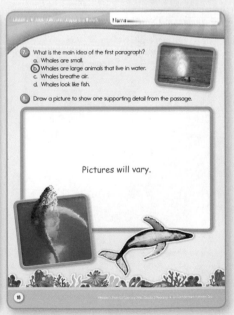

Pictures will vary.

18

Lesson 3

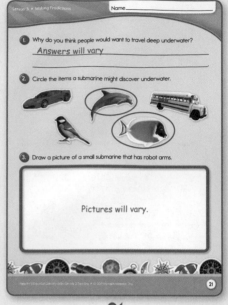

1. Why do you think people would want to travel deep underwater?
<u>Answers will vary</u>

2. Circle the items a submarine might discover underwater.

3. Draw a picture of a small submarine that has robot arms.

Pictures will vary.

21

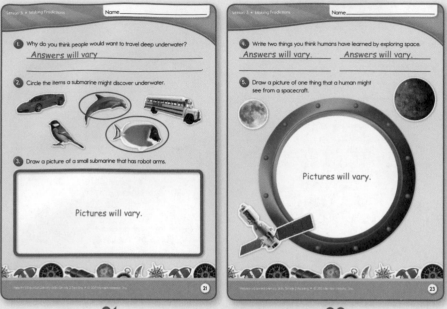

4. Write two things you think humans have learned by exploring space.
<u>Answers will vary.</u>   <u>Answers will vary.</u>

5. Draw a picture of one thing that a human might see from a spacecraft.

Pictures will vary.

23

6. Circle the picture of what an astronaut might wear outside a spacecraft.

7. Why do you think astronauts bring their own oxygen to space?
a. because they have a lot of room on their spacecraft
(b) because there is no oxygen in space
c. because their space suits are heavy

8. Write two other things an astronaut might take into space.
<u>Answers will vary.</u>   <u>Answers will vary.</u>

24

Lesson 4

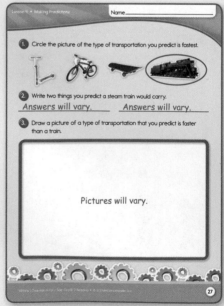

1. Circle the picture of the type of transportation you predict is fastest.

2. Write two things you predict a steam train would carry.
<u>Answers will vary.</u>   <u>Answers will vary.</u>

3. Draw a picture of a type of transportation that you predict is faster than a train.

Pictures will vary.

27

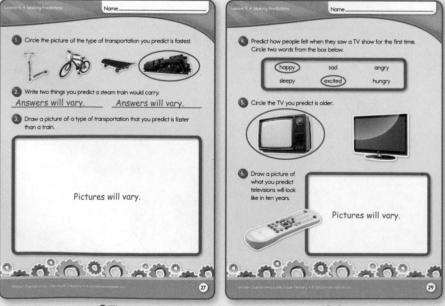

4. Predict how people felt when they saw a TV show for the first time. Circle two words from the box below.

| happy | sad | angry |
| sleepy | excited | hungry |

5. Circle the TV you predict is older.

6. Draw a picture of what you predict televisions will look like in ten years.

Pictures will vary.

29

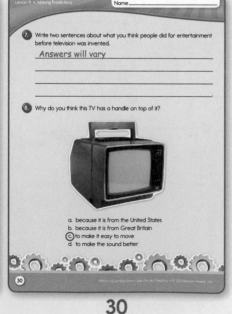

7. Write two sentences about what you think people did for entertainment before television was invented.
<u>Answers will vary</u>

8. Why do you think this TV has a handle on top of it?

a. because it is from the United States
b. because it is from Great Britain
(c) to make it easy to move
d. to make the sound better

30

Lesson 5

(Page 33)

Lesson 5 • Fact and Opinion   Name_____

1. Which sentence is an opinion?
   a. Asia is a beautiful place to visit.
   b. Asian Americans have ancestors that came from Asia.
   c. Many Asian Americans moved to the United States from Asia.
   d. Some Asian Americans have come from China, India, and Japan.

2. Write one fact from paragraph two.
   __Answers will vary__

3. Write an opinion about the picture.
   __Answers will vary__

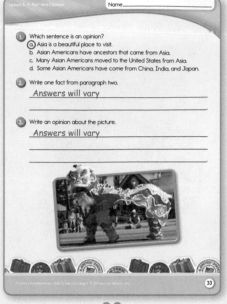

33

(Page 35)

Lesson 5 • Fact and Opinion   Name_____

4. Draw a line between each sentence and its correct description.

   Hispanic Americans have had different reasons for moving to the United States.

   The United States is the best place to find jobs.

   Hispanic Americans are descendants of people who spoke Spanish.

   Hispanic Americans should be very proud of their roots.

   Fact

   Opinion

5. Draw a picture showing one or more facts from the passage.

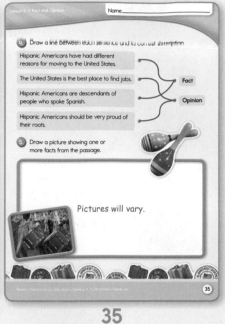

   Pictures will vary.

35

(Page 36)

Lesson 5 • Fact and Opinion   Name_____

6. Circle the fact and underline the opinion.
   • Poverty is another way of saying very poor.
   • Poverty makes everyone unhappy.

7. Look at the map. Circle the areas where the ancestors of Mexican Americans lived.

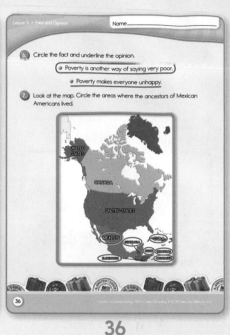

36

Lesson 6

(Page 39)

Lesson 6 • Fact and Opinion   Name_____

1. Draw a line to match each sentence with its correct description.

   Thanksgiving dinner is delicious.   **Fact**

   Thanksgiving is a holiday.   **Opinion**

2. Which statement is a fact?
   a. Everyone loves Thanksgiving.
   b. Playing football is the best thing to do on Thanksgiving.
   c. The United States celebrates Thanksgiving in November.
   d. Turkey is the best thing to eat on Thanksgiving.

3. Draw a picture showing something that people do on Thanksgiving.

   Pictures will vary.

39

(Page 41)

Lesson 6 • Fact and Opinion   Name_____

4. Draw a picture showing one fact from the passage.

   Pictures will vary.

5. Write an opinion about this picture.

   Answers will vary

41

(Page 42)

Lesson 6 • Fact and Opinion   Name_____

6. Which word from the passage means "loud"?
   __noisy__

7. Circle the fact. Underline the opinion.
   • January 1 is when many people celebrate New Year's Day.
   • New Year's Day is a good time to make a resolution.

8. Write one fact from the passage.
   __Answers will vary__

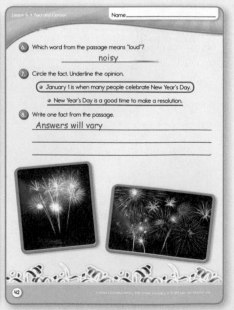

42

Lesson 7

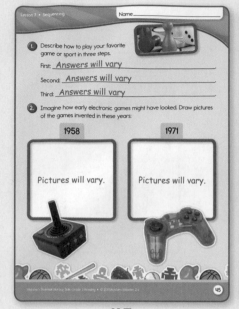

Lesson 7 • Sequencing   Name_____

1. Describe how to play your favorite game or sport in three steps.

First: _Answers will vary_

Second: _Answers will vary_

Third: _Answers will vary_

2. Imagine how early electronic games might have looked. Draw pictures of the games invented in these years:

1958

Pictures will vary.

1971

Pictures will vary.

45

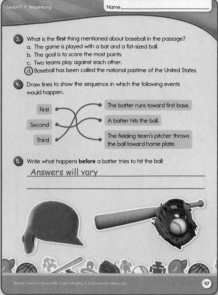

Lesson 7 • Sequencing   Name_____

3. What is the **first** thing mentioned about baseball in the passage?
   a. The game is played with a bat and a fist-sized ball.
   b. The goal is to score the most points.
   c. Two teams play against each other.
   (d.) Baseball has been called the national pastime of the United States.

4. Draw lines to show the sequence in which the following events would happen.

First — A batter hits the ball.

Second — The fielding team's pitcher throws the ball toward home plate.

Third — The batter runs toward first base.

5. Write what happens **before** a batter tries to hit the ball:
   Answers will vary

47

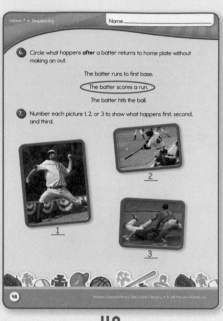

Lesson 7 • Sequencing   Name_____

6. Circle what happens **after** a batter returns to home plate without making an out.

The batter runs to first base.

(The batter scores a run.)

The batter hits the ball.

7. Number each picture 1, 2, or 3 to show what happens first, second, and third.

_1_   _2_   _3_

48

Lesson 8

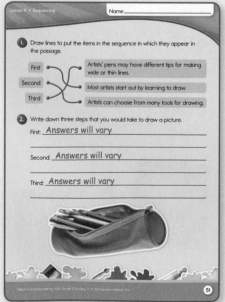

Lesson 8 • Sequencing   Name_____

1. Draw lines to put the items in the sequence in which they appear in the passage.

First — Most artists start out by learning to draw.

Second — Artists can choose from many tools for drawing.

Third — Artists' pens may have different tips for making wide or thin lines.

2. Write down three steps that you would take to draw a picture.

First: _Answers will vary_

Second: _Answers will vary_

Third: _Answers will vary_

51

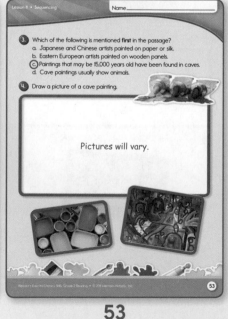

Lesson 8 • Sequencing   Name_____

3. Which of the following is mentioned **first** in the passage?
   a. Japanese and Chinese artists painted on paper or silk.
   b. Eastern European artists painted on wooden panels.
   (c.) Paintings that may be 15,000 years old have been found in caves.
   d. Cave paintings usually show animals.

4. Draw a picture of a cave painting.

Pictures will vary.

53

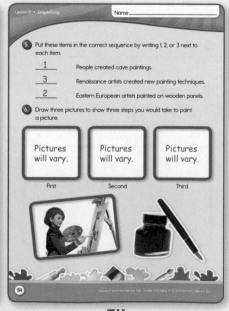

Lesson 8 • Sequencing   Name_____

5. Put these items in the correct sequence by writing 1, 2, or 3 next to each item.

_1_   People created cave paintings.

_3_   Renaissance artists created new painting techniques.

_2_   Eastern European artists painted on wooden panels.

6. Draw three pictures to show three steps you would take to paint a picture.

Pictures will vary.   Pictures will vary.   Pictures will vary.

First   Second   Third

54

Lesson 9

Page 57

1. Read the **cause** and write the **effect**.
   Cause: Plains Indians did not have horses.
   Effect: _Indians hunted on foot_

2. Read the two **effects** and write the correct **cause**.

   Plains Indians got horses brought to the New World by the Spanish.

   Plains Indians were able to travel farther than before.

   Plains Indians were able to kill buffalo more efficiently.

57

Page 59

3. For each **cause** below, choose the correct **effect** from the box. Write the **effect** next to its **cause**.

   The Eskimo made homes from blocks of snow.
   The Eskimo made clothing out of animal fur and sealskin.

Cause	Effect
The Eskimo lived in a very cold part of the world.	The Eskimo made homes from blocks of snow
The Eskimo hunted different kinds of animals.	The Eskimo made clothing out of animal fur and sealskin

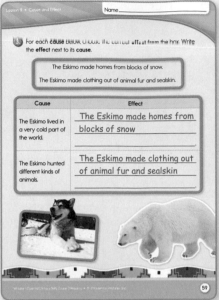

59

Page 60

4. The passage says, "The Eskimo of Alaska had early contact with Russians. Meeting new people changed the Eskimo way of life." Draw two pictures to show the effects that meeting new people had on Eskimo people's lives.

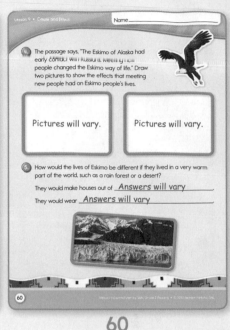

   Pictures will vary.   Pictures will vary.

5. How would the lives of Eskimo be different if they lived in a very warm part of the world, such as a rain forest or a desert?

   They would make houses out of _Answers will vary_
   They would wear _Answers will vary_

60

Lesson 10

Page 63

1. From what source do mechanical clocks get power?
   a. the sun
   b. moving weights or springs
   c. batteries

2. Pick the correct effect from the box and write it on the blank line to complete the sentence.

   the clock to be beautiful   the hands to move   the clock to stop

   The moving gears in a mechanical clock cause _the hands to move_

3. If a mechanical clock is not wound up, what will happen?
   a. Time will speed up.
   b. The clock will stop working.
   c. The hands will move slowly.

4. Draw a picture of a mechanical clock.

   Pictures will vary.

5. Draw a picture of an electrical clock.

   Pictures will vary.

63

Page 65

6. What **effect** does the sun have on a sundial? Underline the correct answer.

   It makes the sundial look old.   It makes a shadow on the sundial.

7. Draw a picture that shows what causes a sundial to work.

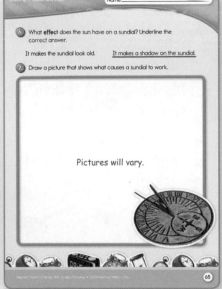

   Pictures will vary.

65

Page 66

8. If there are no shadows on a sundial, what is the **cause**? Underline the correct answer.

   The sun is bright.   The sundial's gears are broken.
   The sun is not shining.   The sundial needs to be wound up.

9. Tell a family member or a friend how these two pictures are the same and how they are different.

   Answers will vary.

   Answers will vary.

66

Lesson 11

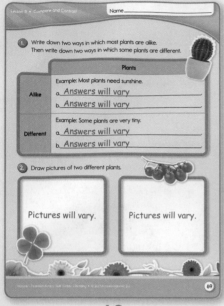

1. Write down two ways in which most plants are alike. Then write down two ways in which some plants are different.

Plants

Alike	Example: Most plants need sunshine. a. _Answers will vary_ b. _Answers will vary_
Different	Example: Some plants are very tiny. a. _Answers will vary_ b. _Answers will vary_

2. Draw pictures of two different plants.

Pictures will vary.

Pictures will vary.

69

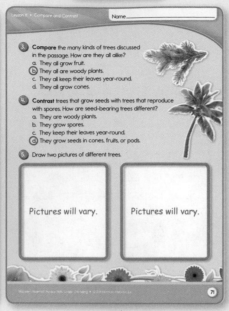

3. **Compare** the many kinds of trees discussed in the passage. How are they all alike?
   a. They all grow fruit.
   (b) They all are woody plants.
   c. They all keep their leaves year-round.
   d. They all grow cones.

4. **Contrast** trees that grow seeds with trees that reproduce with spores. How are seed-bearing trees different?
   a. They are woody plants.
   b. They grow spores.
   c. They keep their leaves year-round.
   (d) They grow seeds in cones, fruits, or pods.

5. Draw two pictures of different trees.

Pictures will vary.

Pictures will vary.

71

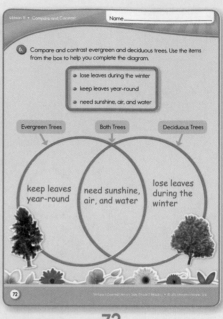

6. Compare and contrast evergreen and deciduous trees. Use the items from the box to help you complete the diagram.

- lose leaves during the winter
- keep leaves year-round
- need sunshine, air, and water

Evergreen Trees — Both Trees — Deciduous Trees

keep leaves year-round

need sunshine, air, and water

lose leaves during the winter

72

Lesson 12

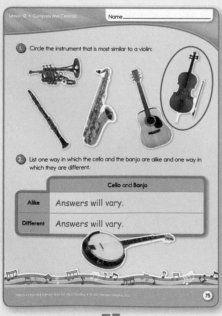

1. Circle the instrument that is most similar to a violin:

2. List one way in which the cello and the banjo are alike and one way in which they are different.

Cello and Banjo

Alike	Answers will vary.
Different	Answers will vary.

75

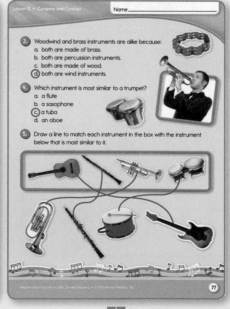

3. Woodwind and brass instruments are alike because:
   a. both are made of brass.
   b. both are percussion instruments.
   c. both are made of wood.
   (d) both are wind instruments.

4. Which instrument is most similar to a trumpet?
   a. a flute
   b. a saxophone
   (c) a tuba
   d. an oboe

5. Draw a line to match each instrument in the box with the instrument below that is most similar to it.

77

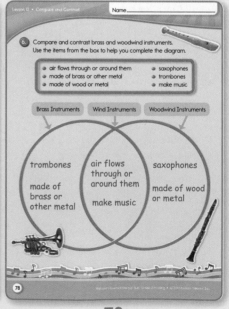

6. Compare and contrast brass and woodwind instruments. Use the items from the box to help you complete the diagram.

- air flows through or around them
- made of brass or other metal
- made of wood or metal
- saxophones
- trombones
- make music

Brass Instruments — Wind Instruments — Woodwind Instruments

trombones

made of brass or other metal

air flows through or around them

make music

saxophones

made of wood or metal

78

Lesson 13

Lesson 13 • Summarizing   Name_____

1. Which sentence best summarizes paragraph one?
   a. Crows are birds that have large families.
   b. Crows like to steal keys and other shiny things.
   (c) Crows are known as smart and curious birds.
   d. Crows are afraid of scarecrows.

2. Summarize paragraph two in one sentence.
   Answers will vary

3. Write two sentences to summarize what you think is happening in the picture.

Answers will vary

81

Lesson 13 • Summarizing   Name_____

4. Summarize paragraph one in one sentence.
   Answers will vary

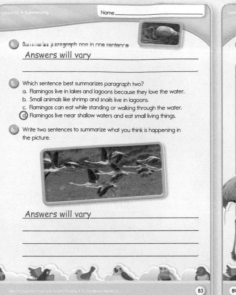

5. Which sentence best summarizes paragraph two?
   a. Flamingos live in lakes and lagoons because they love the water.
   b. Small animals like shrimp and snails live in lagoons.
   c. Flamingos can eat while standing or walking through the water.
   (d) Flamingos live near shallow waters and eat small living things.

6. Write two sentences to summarize what you think is happening in the picture.

Answers will vary

83

Lesson 13 • Summarizing   Name_____

7. Draw a picture that matches the following summary of the passage: "Flamingos are long-legged pink birds that get their food from lagoons."

Pictures will vary.

84

Lesson 14

Lesson 14 • Summarizing   Name_____

1. Which sentence summarizes paragraph one?
   a. Butterflies and moths are insects.
   b. Moths are flying insects.
   (c) Thousands of different flying insects are called butterflies and moths.
   d. Butterflies change forms during their lives.

2. Summarize paragraph two in two sentences.
   Answers will vary

3. Circle the picture of what a butterfly looks like before it is a pupa.

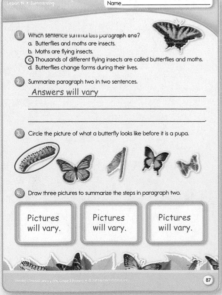

4. Draw three pictures to summarize the steps in paragraph two.

| Pictures will vary. | Pictures will vary. | Pictures will vary. |

87

Lesson 14 • Summarizing   Name_____

5. Which sentence best summarizes paragraph two?
   (a) Most spiders use venom that is usually not harmful to humans.
   b. Spider venom can kill a human.
   c. Spiders shoot venom into their prey.
   d. Some spiders hunt, and others make webs to catch prey.

6. Write two sentences to summarize what you think is happening in the picture.

Answers will vary

89

Lesson 14 • Summarizing   Name_____

7. Draw a picture that summarizes paragraph three.

Pictures will vary.

90

Lesson 15

93

Lesson 15 • Asking Questions   Name_____

1. Write two questions that you have about fairies after reading the passage. Do not forget to put a question mark (?) after each question.
   Answers will vary.

2. What would you ask if you could speak with a fairy? Fill in the blanks with questions.
   Why **Answers will vary.**
   How **Answers will vary.**

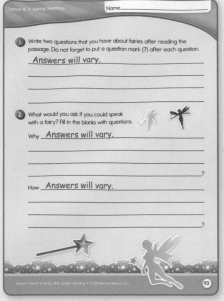

95

Lesson 15 • Asking Questions   Name_____

3. Write two questions that you have after reading the passage. Do not forget to put a question mark (?) after each question.
   Answers will vary.

4. Circle the creature that is believed to live in a lake.
   yeti   sea serpent   [Loch Ness monster]   mermaid

5. Where is the Abominable Snowman believed to live?
   a. northwestern United States
   b. Himalayan mountains
   c. Antarctica
   d. western Canada

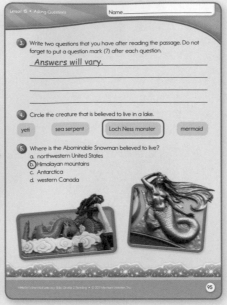

96

Lesson 15 • Asking Questions   Name_____

6. Draw a picture of what you think Bigfoot might look like.

   Pictures will vary.

7. Fill in the blanks with questions about any of the creatures in the passage.
   Why **Answers will vary.**
   How **Answers will vary.**

Lesson 16

99

Lesson 16 • Asking Questions   Name_____

1. Write two questions that you have about nurses after reading the passage. Do not forget to write a question mark (?) after each question.
   Answers will vary.

2. Draw a picture of a nurse at work.

   Pictures will vary.

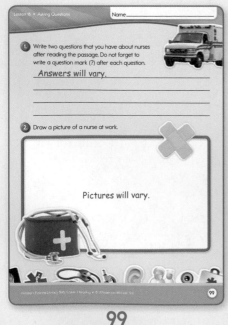

101

Lesson 16 • Asking Questions   Name_____

3. Which of the following is **not** a question?
   a. What is another name for a physician?
   b. How do doctors find out what is making a person sick?
   c. Doctors try to prevent illnesses.
   d. Where do doctors usually work?

4. Draw a line to match each question with its correct answer.

   Question: Answer:
   What is the science of keeping people healthy and healing the sick? — doctor
   What is another name for a physician? — illnesses
   What do doctors try to prevent? — medicine

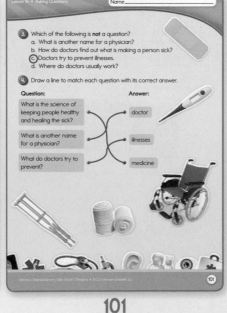

102

Lesson 16 • Asking Questions   Name_____

5. Fill in the blank lines with questions that you would ask a doctor.
   Why **Answers will vary.**
   How **Answers will vary.**

6. Write one question about each picture.
   Answers will vary.   **Answers will vary.**

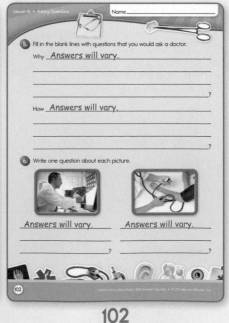

Lesson 17

Lesson 17 • Drawing Conclusions   Name_____

1. What conclusion can you draw about the sun?
   a. The sun is very important to Earth.
   b. The sun is cold.
   c. The sun is tiny.
   d. Earth is the center of the solar system.

2. Write a sentence to describe the picture.

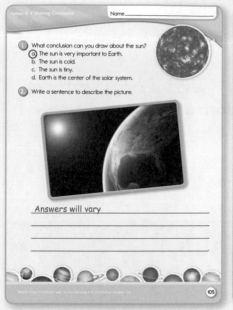

Answers will vary
_____
_____
_____

105

Lesson 17 • Drawing Conclusions   Name_____

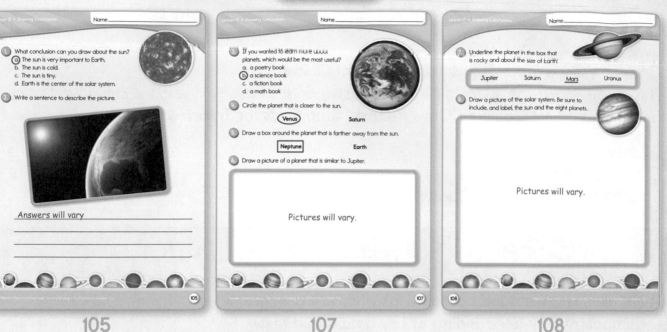

3. If you wanted to learn more about planets, which would be the most useful?
   a. a poetry book
   b. a science book
   c. a fiction book
   d. a math book

4. Circle the planet that is closer to the sun.
   Venus   Saturn

5. Draw a box around the planet that is farther away from the sun.
   Neptune   Earth

6. Draw a picture of a planet that is similar to Jupiter.

Pictures will vary.

107

Lesson 17 • Drawing Conclusions   Name_____

7. Underline the planet in the box that is rocky and about the size of Earth.

   Jupiter   Saturn   Mars   Uranus

8. Draw a picture of the solar system. Be sure to include, and label, the sun and the eight planets.

Pictures will vary.

108

Lesson 18

Lesson 18 • Drawing Conclusions   Name_____

1. Circle the season that is usually colder.
   winter   spring

2. Underline the item you are likely to see in the spring.
   new leaves on trees   hibernating animals   plants that are dying

3. Write the season under each picture.

autumn   winter

111

Lesson 18 • Drawing Conclusions   Name_____

4. Draw a picture of something you might do in the summer.

Pictures will vary.

5. Draw a picture of something you might see in the autumn.

Pictures will vary.

113

Lesson 18 • Drawing Conclusions   Name_____

6. Look at the picture and circle the correct season.

   summer   autumn

7. Circle the season in which you might see or use each item.

   summer   summer
   autumn   autumn

   summer   summer
   autumn   autumn

114

Appendix

Common Core State Standards Alignment Guide
This guide shows the specific alignment between the activity questions in this workbook and the Grade 2 **Common Core Reading Standards for Informational Text**.

L = Lesson
Q = Question
Example: L1Q1 = Lesson 1, Question 1

Key Ideas and Details

Ask and answer such questions as who, what, where, when, why, and how to demonstrate understanding of key details in a text.

L3Q1, L3Q7
L5Q3
L6Q2
L10Q1, L10Q3, L10Q6, L10Q8
L12Q3, L12Q4

L13Q1, L13Q5
L14Q1
L15Q1, L15Q2, L15Q3, L15Q4, L15Q5, L15Q7
L16Q1, L16Q3, L16Q5, L16Q6

Identify the main topic of a multiparagraph text as well as the focus of specific paragraphs within the text.

L1Q1
L2Q3, L2Q7
L5Q2

L13Q2
L14Q2, L14Q5, L14Q7

Describe the connection between a series of historical events, scientific ideas or concepts, or steps in technical procedures in a text.

L2Q6
L7Q1, L7Q4, L7Q7
L8Q1, L8Q2, L8Q5

L9Q1
L16Q4
L17Q7

Craft and Structure

Determine the meaning of words and phrases in a text relevant to a *grade 2 topic or subject area.*

L1Q3

L3Q4

L4Q4

L5Q1, L5Q4

L6Q3, L6Q4, L6Q5, L6Q6

L10Q2

L17Q1

L18Q4, L18Q5

Know and use various text features (e.g., captions, bold print, subheadings, glossaries, indexes, electronic menus, icons) to locate key facts or information in a text efficiently.

L5Q7

L7Q3, L7Q5, L7Q6

L8Q3

L9Q3

L13Q7

Identify the main purpose of a text, including what the author wants to answer, explain, or describe.

L1Q4, L1Q7

L2Q1

L4Q6

L13Q4

L17Q1

L18Q2

Integration of Knowledge and Ideas

Explain how specific images (e.g., a diagram showing how a machine works) contribute to and clarify a text.

L1Q6	L12Q1, L12Q6
L2Q5	L13Q3, L13Q6
L3Q2, L3Q6	L14Q3, L14Q6
L4Q1, L4Q5	L17Q4, L17Q5
L9Q2	L18Q3
L11Q7	

Describe how reasons support specific points the author makes in a text.

L1Q2, L1Q5	L6Q1, L6Q7, L6Q8
L2Q2	L11Q1
L3Q8	L12Q2
L4Q2, L4Q7, L4Q8	L17Q3
L5Q5, L5Q6	L18Q6

Compare and contrast the most important points presented by two texts on the same topic.

L9Q5	L12Q5
L10Q9	L17Q8
L11Q4, L11Q5	L18Q7

Range of Reading and Level of Text Complexity

By the end of year, read and comprehend informational texts, including history/social studies, science, and technical texts, in the grades 2–3 text complexity band proficiently, with scaffolding as needed at the high end of the range.

This learning standard is addressed, in different ways, through each of the 18 lessons.

More information about the Common Core State Standards can be found at www.corestandards.org

Britannica Elementary Encyclopedia Sources

The 18 lessons within the **Webster's Essential Literacy Skills** workbooks are based on nonfiction passages taken from the *Britannica Student Encyclopedia*. These passages can be found online in the Britannica Elementary Encyclopedia section of the *Britannica Online School Edition* at school.eb.com. Information on subscribing to the *Britannica Online School Edition* or other Britannica sites can be found at info.eb.com.

Lesson 1: Farm Animals	**Horse:** http://school.eb.com/elementary/article?articleId=353265
	Chicken: http://school.eb.com/elementary/article?articleId=352949
	Pig: http://school.eb.com/elementary/article?articleId=353626
Lesson 2: Ocean Animals	**Sea Star:** http://school.eb.com/elementary/article?articleId=353809
	Shark: http://school.eb.com/elementary/article?articleId=353766
	Whale: http://school.eb.com/elementary/article?articleId=353922
Lesson 3: Explorers and Explorations	**Christopher Columbus:** http://school.eb.com/elementary/article?articleId=352985
	Submarine: http://school.eb.com/elementary/article?articleId=390261
	Space Exploration: http://school.eb.com/elementary/article?articleId=353794
Lesson 4: Inventors and Inventions	**Thomas Alva Edison:** http://school.eb.com/elementary/article?articleId=353084
	Railroad: http://school.eb.com/elementary/article?articleId=353694
	Television: http://www.school.eb.com/elementary/article?articleId=353844
Lesson 5: Immigration	**Ellis Island:** http://school.eb.com/elementary/article?articleId=399857
	Asian Americans: http://school.eb.com/elementary/article?articleId=352792
	Hispanic Americans: http://school.eb.com/elementary/article?articleId=353253
Lesson 6: Celebrations	**Cinco de Mayo:** http://school.eb.com/elementary/article?articleId=352963
	Thanksgiving: http://school.eb.com/elementary/article?articleId=353852
	New Year's Day: http://school.eb.com/elementary/article?articleId=353529
Lesson 7: Sports and Games	**Basketball:** http://school.eb.com/elementary/article?articleId=352831
	Electronic Games: http://school.eb.com/elementary/article?articleId=400103
	Baseball: http://school.eb.com/elementary/article?articleId=352829
Lesson 8: Works of Art	**Sculpture:** http://school.eb.com/elementary/article?articleId=353751
	Drawing: http://school.eb.com/elementary/article?articleId=390735
	Painting: http://school.eb.com/elementary/article?articleId=353589

Lesson 9: Native Americans	**Native Americans:** http://school.eb.com/elementary/article?articleId=353288
	Plains Indians: http://school.eb.com/elementary/article?articleId=353637
	Eskimo: http://school.eb.com/elementary/article?articleId=353295

Lesson 10: Time	**Time:** http://school.eb.com/elementary/article?articleId=353860
	Clock: http://school.eb.com/elementary/article?articleId=400097
	Sundial: http://school.eb.com/elementary/article?articleId=403911

Lesson 11: Flowers, Plants, and Trees	**Flower:** http://school.eb.com/elementary/article?articleId=353137
	Plant: http://school.eb.com/elementary/article?articleId=353639
	Tree: http://school.eb.com/elementary/article?articleId=399629

| Lesson 12: Musical Instruments | **Musical Instrument:** http://school.eb.com/elementary/article?articleId=353508 |

Lesson 13: Birds	**Owl:** http://school.eb.com/elementary/article?articleId=353584
	Crow: http://school.eb.com/elementary/article?articleId=353020
	Flamingo: http://school.eb.com/elementary/article?articleId=353133

Lesson 14: Insects and Spiders	**Firefly:** http://school.eb.com/elementary/article?articleId=353129
	Butterfly and Moth: http://school.eb.com/elementary/article?articleId=352890
	Spider: http://school.eb.com/elementary/article?articleId=353800

| Lesson 15: Legendary Creatures | **Legendary Animals:** http://school.eb.com/elementary/article?articleId=352758 |
| | **Irish Folklore:** http://school.eb.com/elementary/article?articleId=488146 |

Lesson 16: Medical Jobs	**Dentistry:** http://school.eb.com/elementary/article?articleId=390724
	Nursing: http://school.eb.com/elementary/article?articleId=353552
	Medicine: http://school.eb.com/elementary/article?articleId=353448

Lesson 17: The Solar System	**Solar System:** http://school.eb.com/elementary/article?articleId=353789
	Sun: http://school.eb.com/elementary/article?articleId=353824
	Planets: http://school.eb.com/elementary/article?articleId=353638

| Lesson 18: Seasons | **Season:** http://school.eb.com/elementary/article?articleId=399589 |